My Feelings Workbook

A Workbook For Teaching Children About Feelings and Developing Emotional Intelligence

Grades 1-5

by: Aaron Wiemeier, M.S. LPC

Illustrated by: Karla Trapp

© 2011 by YouthLight, Inc. | Chapin, SC 29036

All rights reserved. Permission is given for individuals to reproduce the worksheets in this book. Reproduction of any other material is strictly prohibited.

Layout and Design by Melody Taylor

Project Editing by Susan Bowman

Library of Congress Control Number
2010941469

ISBN
978-1-59850-095-0

10 9 8 7 6 5 4 3 2 1
Printed in the United States

Table of Contents

I. Overview 4
   Rationale 5

II. Suggestions for Counselors 6

III. **About Me and My Body**
   Personal Information 8
   About My Body 9
   Body Rainbow Exercise 10

III. **Feelings**
   Feelings: What Are They? Where Are They? 11
   The Big 5 Feelings 13
   Our Feeling Friends & Activities 15
   Feeling Group 1: Sammy "The Sad" Sheep 18
   Feeling Group 2: Marvin "The Mad" 25
   Feeling Group 3: Sara "The Scared" Seahorse 39
   Feeling Group 4: Ella "The Excited" Elephant 46
   Feeling Group 5: Rusty: The Relaxed" Rabbit 53

IV. **Dealing With Feelings**
   Feelings: Making a Right or Wrong Choice 62
   Right Choices: Coping Skill Development 63
   My Healing Hand 68
   Feelings: Putting It All Together 69
   My Feelings Traffic Light 72
   My Feelings Train 73

V. **Fun Feeling Activities**
   Feelings Word Search 75
   Feelings Crossword 76
   Anger True False Quiz 77
   Feelings Quiz 78

VI. School Tools
- Activity 1 - Movie Night 79
- Activity 2 - Magazine Magic 81
- Activity 3 - Picture Day 82
- Activity 4 - New Feelings Practice 83
- Activity 5 - Touchy Feely 85
- Activity 6 - Feelings Collage 86
- Activity 7 - Feel the Music 87
- Activity 8 - Feelings Charades 88
- Activity 9 - Build a Feeling 90

VII. Appendices
- My Feelings Chart 91
- Where I Feel Things in My Body 92
- My Anger Thermometer 93
- My Healing Hand Story 94
- My Feelings Traffic Light 99
- My Feelings Train 100

VIII. Additional
- Answers to Crossword And Quizzes 102
- About the Author 103
- References 104

Overview

This book is divided into 4 main sections and includes the following:

Section 1: *Body Awareness and Feelings* – This section includes activities and information related to helping children understand what feelings are, where they might feel them in their body, and debunks some basic myths about feelings. It also helps categorize aspects of feelings for children in a way they can more easily grasp and identify in the future.

Section 2: *In Depth about Feelings* – This section goes in depth to provide critical information about the 5 most common feelings children have. It is filled with activities, sentence completion and fill in the blank activities to make learning more fun and engaging for the child.

Section 3: *Coping Skill Development* – This section helps children differentiate between right and wrong decisions surrounding feelings and helps identify things they can do when they feel certain ways to help them cope. This section is filled with fun activities as well.

Section 4: *Lesson Plans, Activities and Tools* – This section provides lesson plan ideas incorporating sections 1-3 for educators, counselors and parents for either individual or group instruction. It also includes reproducible worksheets.

Rationale

It is widely researched and studied that trauma in all its forms has a profound impact on the developing brain and body (Bremner et al., 1997). More specifically, developmental trauma, which can be chronic everyday stress, can have the same impact on the brain as a single episode of acute trauma such as a car crash (DeAngelis, 2007; Trauma, Brain & Relationship, 2004). Developmental trauma decreases a child's ability to calm and soothe themselves in the face of stress, challenge or difficulty (De Bellis et al., 1994). Additionally, one of the common symptoms of Post-traumatic stress disorder is a generalized numbing of body sensation and awareness, thus contributing to poor affect regulation and awareness since feelings are felt and trauma is stored in the body (Volpicelli et al., 1999). Simply stated, a child's emotional self is markedly affected by even moderate levels of stress.

Adding to this problem are general misperceptions and distortions about emotions and feelings both culturally and in relation to gender. For example, the most common question asked when someone is upset is how they feel, giving no credence to the most important aspect of where they feel. Another misperception is the idea that other people make you angry, which teaches children at a young age to displace responsibility for their actions around anger on to others. Males are also often encouraged to believe that feeling sad or crying is bad or wrong in some way (Doka and Martin, 2000). These types of beliefs enhance the propensity that children will have poor awareness of their emotional self and thus a lessened capacity to handle stressful situations.

The purpose of this workbook is to teach children the many aspects of emotions and feelings including the awareness of where they feel things in their body. This awareness when paired with an acquisition of coping skills, can help children feel confident to handle and manage the stresses that occur in their lives. More specifically, teaching children where they feel feelings in their body can serve as a bridge between the cerebral cortex or thinking mind and the emotional mind or limbic brain. Since trauma memory is often locked within the limbic brain as sensory or non-declarative memory, learning to focus on where you feel things in your body can help the processing of traumatic events and stress within the brain and body (Van Der Kolk, 2004).

Suggestions for Counselors

1. You can laminate any of the appendices and reuse them with dry erase markers. Children need to practice the concepts in this workbook many times over for it to really sink in.

2. You can also laminate two versions of feelings faces to help with the identification of feelings (You can get these online by typing the words "feeling faces" into your search engine).

3. For little children who cannot yet read, I would use icons where appropriate (for example in the boxes on Appendix F or above the fingers on the Healing Hand). They are more likely to effectively identify & use the coping skills this way.

4. Make it fun. Practice should occur when the child is in a positive mood, not just when they are angry. For Example; watch a children's movie and have your child identify what a certain character feels and WHERE they feel it in their body. Or to help with descriptions of feelings, use different substances like having your child put their hand in jello and describe how, where and how strong the feeling is (refer to the School Tools Section & Appendix A & B of this book).

5. This workbook is developmentally suitable for kids up to approximately 10 years of age, although there is no definite age at which it cannot be used depending on developmental and emotional maturity.

6. Throughout this workbook there are Lesson Objective notes. These are meant to give guidance to the parent, teacher or counselor as to the function and goals of that particular activity.

Note: If you do not feel comfortable using this workbook, refrain from doing so and consult a professional mental health clinician to assist you. The creator of this workbook shall in no way be liable for the misuse of materials herein.

My FEELINGS Workbook

Name: _____

*"Today I'll stand up tall and say;
ALL MY FEELINGS are okay"*

About Me

My Full Name is _____

I am _____ years old

My birthday is _____

I live with/in _____

I like _____

_____

I do not like _____

_____

Something special about me is _____

Draw or paste a picture of you in the box below

About My Body

Lesson 1 Objective: Children will learn how to identify most of the major parts of their bodies.

Just like a rainbow is made up of different colors, our bodies are made up of different parts.

Do you know the PARTS of your body?

Draw a face on child's body according to how you feel and color each part of the body with the correct color to make a BODY RAINBOW!

Ears – Red	**Mouth – Purple**
Head – Yellow	**Knees – Green**
Fingers – Green	**Toes – Red**
Hands – Purple	**Ankles – Blue**
Elbows – Yellow	**Feet – Purple**
Arms – Green	**Legs – Orange**
Eyes – Blue	**Face – Green**
Neck – Orange	**Chest – Blue**
Shoulders – Red	**Pelvis/Hips – Yellow**

© Youthlight, Inc.

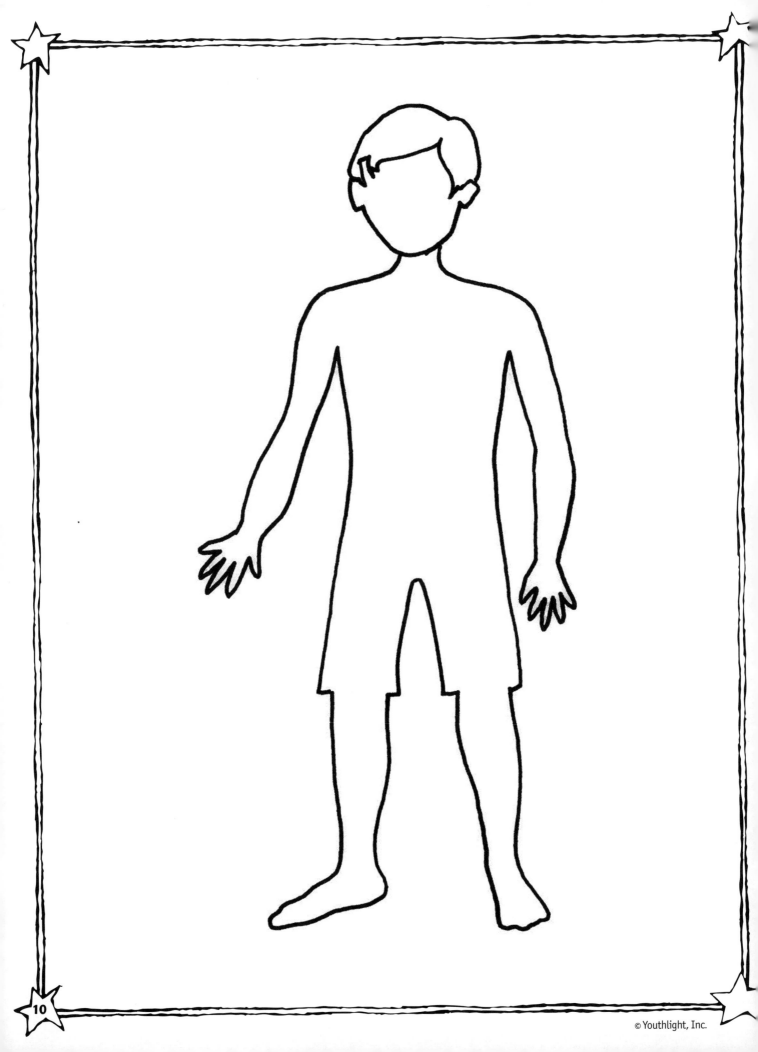

Feelings

Feelings are like the wind. You can't see them but you know they are there. Feelings are the way our bodies make sense of what happens to us in our lives; both good and bad things. Most importantly all feelings are normal and everyone gets them sometimes.

You know you are having a feeling because you feel it on or inside your body!!

Lesson 2 Objective: Children will associate a feeling with where they typically might feel it in their body.

Step 1: Pick a feeling below that you recognize and circle it or color it in.

Step 2: What feeling do you think this is? _____

Step 3: Do you feel this feeling inside your body? _____

    If yes, then where? _____

Step 4: Do you feel this feeling on the outside of your body?

    If yes, then where? _____

Not sure?? That's OK..this is one of the things we will be learning in this workbook!!

Lesson 3 Objective: To see how many feelings, if any, the child already knows.

List or draw some feelings you already know in the box below!

Angry Apple says *Mad, Angry & Frustrated* are the same feeling, just different amounts!

Hint... Hint!!

The Big 5 Feelings

All feelings, no matter what the names are, can be put into 5 main categories or groups.

Our animal friends Sammy the Sheep, Marvin the Moose, Ella the Elephant, Rusty the Rabbit & Sara the Seahorse will help us on our journey to learn about the 5 groups of feelings.

Lesson 4 Objective: Children will learn the 5 categories of feelings and associate those feelings with color.

Step 1: Pick from the feelings list below how you think each of our animal friends is feeling today. Then write that feeling on the line below each animal on the following page.

Sad **Mad** **Excited** **Relaxed** **Scared**

Step 2: Color the animal the color you think they are based on how they are feeling today. Some color choices could be:

Blue **Red** **Green** **Yellow** **Orange**

Sammy the Sheep

_____

Marvin the Moose

_____

Ella the Elephant

_____

Rusty the Rabbit

_____

Sara the Seahorse

_____

© Youthlight, Inc.

Lesson 5 Objective: Children will connect feelings to facial expressions.

Uh oh...Our animal friends have forgotten how they feel today. Remind them by drawing a line from the animal in the left column to the feeling face in the right column that matches how the animal is feeling.

Sammy the Sheep

Marvin the Moose

Ella the Elephant

Rusty the Rabbit

Sara the Seahorse

Lesson 6 Objective: Children will explore how animals might experience feelings.

Just like us, animals experience their feelings in or on their bodies!

Circle the places where you think each of our animal friends feels their feeling and then color those places in on the picture of each animal (you can circle more than one)!

Sammy "The Sad" Sheep

| hooves | shoulders | heart | mouth |

Marvin "The Mad" Moose

| hooves | legs | stomach | eyes |

Ella "The Excited" Elephant

| trunk   skin   ears   tail |

Rusty "The Relaxed" Rabbit

| face   paws   nose   shoulders |

Sara "The Scared" Seahorse

| stomach   tail   eyes   fin |

Feeling Group 1: Sad

Lesson 8 Objective: Children will learn other names for the sad group feelings and to introduce the concept of different amounts of sad.

As Sammy surely knows, there are other feelings in the sad group that are similar to sad, just different amounts of sadness. We can think of these feelings in terms of amounts from 0-10 where 10 is the most you have ever felt, 0 is none at all, and 5 is in the middle (see Appendix A).

Step 1: In the picture, find and color Sammy "the sad" Sheep – she is a number 6!

Step 2: Now color in Sammy's friends and think about if they are more or less sad than Sammy. Look at their bodies. How can you tell if they are more or less sad than Sammy? (Hint: If their number is more than 6, they have more sadness than Sammy. If their number is less than 6 they have less sadness than Sammy.)

EXTRA CREDIT!! If they are more sad, color them darker than Sammy by pressing harder. If they are less sad, color them lighter than Sammy by pressing lighter.

Sean "the distraught" Sheep – I am a number 10

Sally "the lonely" Sheep – I am a number 3

Sergio "the disappointed" Sheep – I am a number 5

Sandra "the depressed" Sheep – I am a number 8

What Does Sad Feel Like?

Hello kids, this is Sammy "the sad" Sheep. When I am feeling sad, this is what it feels like in my body...

It feels heavy like a ton of bricks are on top of my shoulders.

It feels empty like there is a big black hole in my heart.

It feels dark like the light bulb has gone out in my brain.

It feels cold like I am sitting in a bathtub full of ice cubes.
(Draw a picture of this for Sammy below.)

What are the clues that you might be sad?
Sammy says you can tell you might be sad by listening to your body clues. It is important to know if you are sad so you can get help to feel better.

Lesson 9 Objective: Children will learn to identify where they may feel sadness in their body.

Step 1: Finish the sentence below

I felt sad when _____

Step 2: Draw in your sad face. Then check the body clues below if you think you felt it when you were sad.

Step 3: For each body clue checked, color and/or draw a line to where you think it might be on the picture to the right.

__ **Breathe slower**

__ **Stomach hurts**

__ **Talk slower**

__ **Eye lids droop or feel heavy**

__ **Heart slows down**

__ **Jaw loosens**

__ **Eye brows go down**

__ **Shoulders drop**

__ **Mouth frowns**

__ **Weak legs**

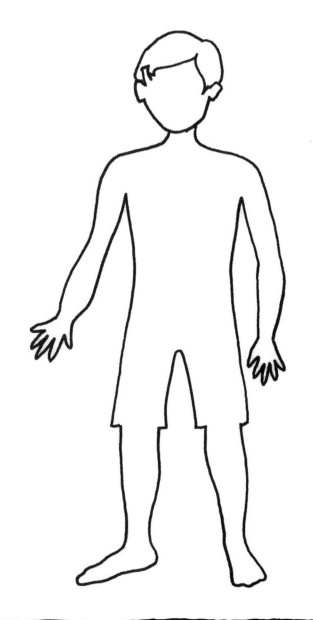

Sammy's Sad Trivia

Sammy "the sad" Sheep says....

1. It is normal to feel sad sometimes and not know why.

2. Sometimes when people feel sad for too long, or they feel they cannot handle the sad feeling, they turn it into another feeling like anger.

3. Not all people feel sad when they lose someone they love. Some cultures celebrate the death of a relative.

4. Crying is a normal way the body heals itself when you feel sad. Holding in your tears may actually make you more sad.

5. After feeling sad for a long period of time, you often feel exhausted because your body uses up so much energy feeling sad.

6. The sad part of your brain is connected by special cells called nerves to your stomach. This is why many people feel sadness in their stomachs.

7. There is always something you can do when you are feeling sad to help you feel better.

Feeling Sad? What Would You Do?

Lesson 10 Objective: Children will explore where and to what degree their feelings are in certain situations and what they can do about it to feel better.

Fill in the blanks and circle how much sadness you might feel based on the situation (use Appendix A & B).

1. You just found out your best friend is moving to another state.

How much sadness would you feel?   A little   A lot
(Hint: On Appendix A – less than 5 = A little & more than 5 = A lot)

Where would you feel it in your body? _____

What would you do to help you feel better? _____
_____

2. Your parents said you could not go to your friend's birthday party.

How much sadness would you feel?   A little   A lot

Where would you feel it in your body? _____

What would you do to help you feel better? _____
_____

3. You just found out your pet dog died.

How much sadness would you feel?   A little   A lot

Where would you feel it in your body? _____

What would you do to help you feel better? _____
_____

Feeling Group 2: Mad

Lesson 11 Objective: Children will learn other names for the mad group feelings and to introduce the concept of different amounts of mad.

As Marvin surely knows, there are other feelings in the mad group that are similar to mad, just different amounts of madness. We can think of these feelings in terms of amounts from 0-10 where 10 is the most you have ever felt, 0 is none at all, and 5 is in the middle (see Appendix A).

Step 1: In the picture, find and color Marvin "the mad" Moose – he is a number 6!

Step 2: Now color in Marvin's friends and think about if they are more or less mad than Marvin. Look at their bodies. How can you tell if they are more or less mad than Marvin? (Hint: If their number is more than 6, they have more madness than Marvin. If their number is less than 6 they have less madness than Marvin.)

EXTRA CREDIT!! *If they are more mad, color them darker than Marvin by pressing harder. If they are less mad, color them lighter than Marvin by pressing lighter.*

Molly "the raging" Moose – I am a number 10

Michael "the irritated" Moose – I am a number 3

Michelle "the frustrated" Moose – I am a number 5

Mason "the angry" Moose – I am a number 8

What Does Mad Feel Like?

Hello kids, this is Marvin "the mad" Moose. When I am feeling mad, this is what it feels like in my body...

It feels fast like a race car is racing around in my head.

It feels hot like there is a big sun heating up my skin.

© Youthlight, Inc.

It feels tight like my hooves are tied up in knots.

It feels rough like my moose body is covered in sandpaper.
(Draw a picture of this for Marvin below.)

What are the clues that you might be mad?
Marvin says you can tell you might be mad by listening to your body clues. It is important to know if you are mad so you can get help to feel better.

Lesson 12 Objective: Children will learn to identify where they may feel mad in their body.

Step 1: Finish the sentence below

I felt mad when_____

Step 2: Draw in your mad face. Then check the body clues below if you think you felt it when you were mad.

Step 3: For each body clue checked, color and/or draw a line to where you think it might be on the picture to the right.

__ **Muscles tighten up – Body gets stiff**

__ **Face feels hot – cheeks get red**

__ **Breathe faster**

__ **Head hurts – feels full of racing thoughts**

__ **Make fists**

__ **Stomach feels like it's in knots**

__ **Heart pounds**

__ **Jaw & mouth tightens**

__ **Body shakes**

__ **Eye brows furl or go down**

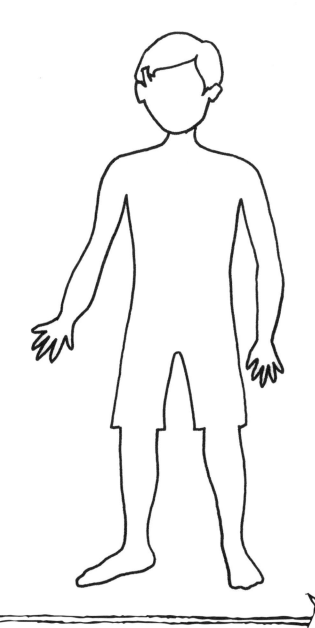

© Youthlight, Inc.

Lesson 13 Objective: To empower children to know they have a choice in whether or not to feel mad and to teach them the most common feeling that precipitates anger.

Psst....Marvin here. There are 2 special things I think you should know about the feeling mad. If there is something I know a lot about it's feeling mad.

*First, no one MAKES us mad. We choose to be mad.

**Second, whenever we feel mad it is really because we are feeling scared or sad or some other feeling underneath.

Uh oh.. another moose just walked off with my food...help me choose to not feel mad by drawing in a smile instead of a frown. Then color me in a cool color like blue, green or brown!

Marvin's Mad Trivia

Marvin "the mad" Moose says....

1. It is normal to feel mad sometimes and not know why.

2. Sometimes when we get very very mad, it's hard to remember things that we did or said when we were mad.

3. No one can make you mad; you choose to become mad.

4. Scared is the feeling that is sometimes underneath mad.

5. It is normal to feel mad sometimes; it is what you do when you are mad that can be wrong.

6. Most often when we feel mad, it is connected to or reminds us of some hurt from our past.

7. We can learn how to be mad from watching others.

8. There is always something you can do when you are feeling mad to help you feel better.

Marvin here....although we feel mad in many different parts of our bodies, we can usually tell when we or someone else is mad by looking at our faces; especially our eyebrows. Do I have eyebrows??

Lesson 14 Objective: Children will learn the power of facial expressions when it comes to telling if they or others are angry.

Practice making your face look mad by moving your eyebrows down towards your nose. Now turn the face below mad by putting downward dashes above the eyes ╲ ╱

Next time you feel mad, what will your face do?

Feeling Mad? What Would You Do?

Lesson 14 Objective: Children will rate their level of feeling mad to the following situations and what they can do about it to feel better.

Fill in the blanks and circle how mad you might feel based on the situation (use Appendix A & B).

1. You just found out your favorite electronic game was broken by your sibling.

How mad would you feel?   A little   A lot
(Hint: On Appendix A – less than 5 = A little & more than 5 = A lot)

Where would you feel it in your body? _____

What would you do to help you feel better? _____
_____

2. You found out your sibling lied to your parent about something you did not do.

How mad would you feel?   A little   A lot

Where would you feel it in your body? _____

What would you do to help you feel better? _____
_____

3. A kid in your class pushed you down on the playground.

How mad would you feel?   A little   A lot

Where would you feel it in your body? _____

What would you do to help you feel better? _____
_____

How Hot Are You?

Marvin says another way to understand the amounts of anger is in terms of temperature. Take a look at Appendix C (Anger Thermometer) in the back of this book to help you. The hotter your temperature the more mad you feel. Sometimes when you get too hot, you may "boil over." Have you ever gotten so mad and hot you boiled over? If so, draw a picture of what happened in the box below!

Lesson 15 Objective: To help kids find alternative ways to understand the amounts of anger based on certain situations.

Refer to Appendix C (Anger Thermometer) in the back of this workbook if needed.

Step 1: Have children write in the temperature below each thermometer on the next page for how hot they would feel in each situation.

Step 2: Then have them color or fill in the thermometer based on how hot they would be for each situation.

1. A kid in your class says you are stupid.

2. Your brother/sister tells your mother you took one of their toys but you did not.

3. Your father says you cannot go out to play unless you clean your room first.

4. Someone steals your favorite toy.

5. Your brother/sister gets to have a piece of candy but you cannot.

6. Your brother/sister gets to stay up later than you and watch television.

7. No one pays attention to you even though you keep raising your hand.

8. You get grounded for not doing your homework.

9. Someone cuts in front of you in line.

10. Your parents say you cannot play with your friends outside after dinner.

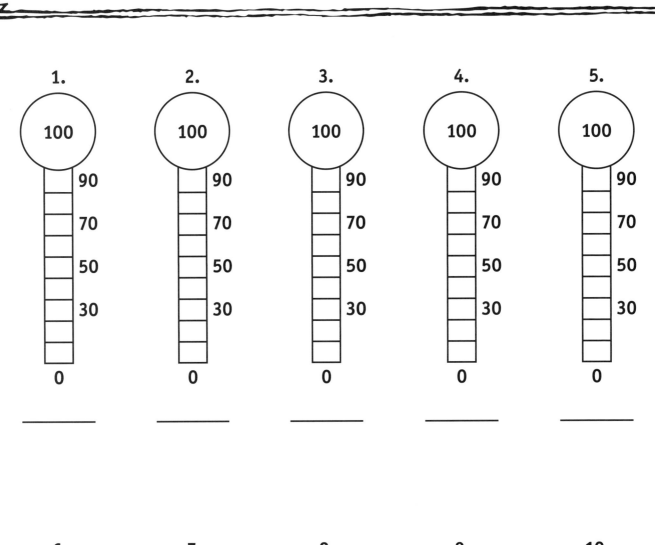

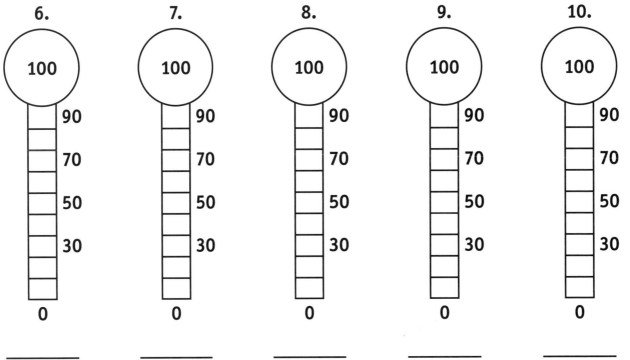

Feeling Group 3: Scared

Lesson 16 Objective: To teach children other names for the scared group feelings and to introduce the concept of different levels of being scared.

As Sara surely knows, there are other feelings in the scared group that are similar to scared, just different amounts of scared. We can think of these feelings in terms of amounts from 0-10 where 10 is the most you have ever felt, 0 is none at all, and 5 is in the middle (see Appendix A).

Step 1: In the picture, find and color Sara "the scared" Seahorse – she is a number 6!

Step 2: Now color in Sara's friends and think about if they are more or less scared than Sara. Look at their bodies. How can you tell if they are more or less scared than Sara? (Hint: If their number is more than 6, they are more scared than Sara. If their number is less than 6 they are less scared than Sara.)

EXTRA CREDIT!! If they are more scared, color them darker than Sara by pressing harder. If they are less scared, color them lighter than Sara by pressing lighter.

Sasha "the terrified" Seahorse – I am a number 10

Steven "the nervous" Seahorse – I am a number 3

Shelly "the anxious" Seahorse – I am a number 5

Skyler "the frightened" Seahorse – I am a number 8

What Does Scared Feel Like?

Hello kids, this is Sara "the scared" Seahorse. When I am feeling scared, this is what it feels like in my body...

It feels sharp like needles on the back of my neck.

It feels fast like a race car driving around inside my chest.

It feels busy like a hundred bees buzzing around my head.

It feels like my fins and tail are on fire and burning.
(Draw a picture of this for Sara below.)

What are the clues that you might be scared?
Sara says you can tell you might be scared by listening to your body clues. It is important to know if you are scared so you can get help to feel better and stay safe.

Lesson 17 Objective: Children will learn to identify where they may feel scared in their body.

Step 1: Finish the sentence below

I felt scared when _____

Step 2: Draw in your scared face. Then check the body clues below if you think you felt it when you were scared.

Step 3: For each body clue checked, color and/or draw a line to where you think it might be on the picture to the right.

__ **Face feels hot – cheeks get red**

__ **Hands & feet feel hot**

__ **Breathe faster**

__ **Feel angry**

__ **Hard to pay attention**

__ **Want to fight or run**

__ **Talk faster**

__ **Stomach feels like it's in knots**

__ **Heart pounds**

__ **Body shakes**

__ **Eye brows go up**

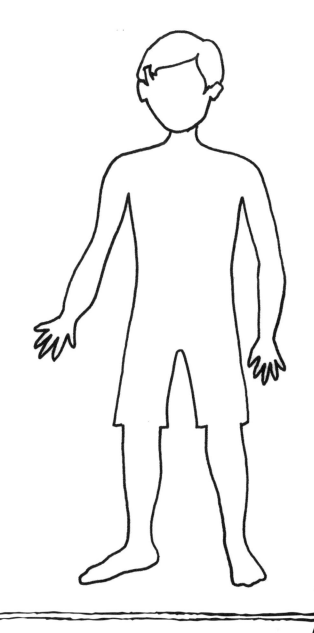

Sara's Scared Trivia

Sara "the scared" Seahorse says....

1. It is normal to feel scared sometimes and not know why.

2. Feeling scared is sometimes a "warning signal" that you may be in danger.

3. Most people are more scared of losing someone they love than of things like snakes and spiders.

4. Sometimes when people are really scared they may run away, freeze in place or fight.

5. Sometimes we feel scared because what is happening now reminds us of something scary that happened in the past.

6. Animals feel scared like us sometimes.

7. When you get scared, your hands and feet may feel warm because your heart is sending more blood to those parts of your body.

8. There is always something you can do when you are feeling scared to help you feel better.

Feeling Scared? What Would You Do?

Lesson 18 Objective: Children will rate their level of scared in certain situations.

Fill in the blanks and circle how scared you might feel based on the situation (use Appendix A & B).

1. You had a bad dream that woke you up in the middle of the night.

How scared would you feel?   A little   A lot
(Hint: On Appendix A – less than 5 = A little & more than 5 = A lot)

Where would you feel it in your body? _____

What would you do to help you feel better? _____
_____

2. You heard your parents arguing loudly in the other room.

How scared would you feel?   A little   A lot

Where would you feel it in your body? _____

What would you do to help you feel better? _____
_____

3. An older and bigger kid at school threatened to beat you up.

How scared would you feel?   A little   A lot

Where would you feel it in your body? _____

What would you do to help you feel better? _____
_____

© Youthlight, Inc.

Feeling Group 4: Excited

Lesson 19 Objective: To teach children other names for the excited group feelings and to introduce the concept of different levels of being excited.

As Ella surely knows, there are other feelings in the excited group that are similar to excited, just different amounts of excited. We can think of these feelings in terms of amounts from 0-10 where 10 is the most you have ever felt, 0 is none at all, and 5 is in the middle (see Appendix A).

Step 1: In the picture, find and color Ella "the excited" Elephant – she is a number 8!

Step 2: Now color in Ella's friends and think about if they are more or less excited than Ella. Look at their bodies. How can you tell if they are more or less excited than Ella? (Hint: If their number is more than 8, they are more excited than Ella. If their number is less than 8, they are less excited than Ella.)

EXTRA CREDIT!! *If they are more excited, color them darker than Ella by pressing harder. If they are less excited, color them lighter than Ella by pressing lighter.*

Eli "the elated" Elephant – I am a number 10

Elizabeth "the energized" Elephant – I am a number 2

Eugene "the happy" Elephant – I am a number 6

Ebony "the glad" Elephant – I am a number 4

What Does Excited Feel Like?

Hello kids, this is Ella "the excited" Elephant. When I am feeling excited, this is what it feels like in my body...

It feels like something is pulling all my legs in different directions.

It feels strong like my trunk could lift a car.

It feels fast like shooting stars inside my chest.

It feels light like my legs are floating off the ground.
(Draw a picture of this for Ella below.)

What are the clues that you might be excited?
Ella says you can tell you might be excited by listening to your body clues. It is important to know if you are excited so you can keep your body in control and not bother others.

Lesson 20 Objective: Children will learn to identify where they may feel excitement in their body.

Step 1: Finish the sentence below

I felt excited when _____

Step 2: Draw in your excited face. Then check the body clues below if you think you felt it when you were excited.

Step 3: For each body clue checked, color and/or draw a line to where you think it might be on the picture to the right.

___ **Face feels hot – cheeks get red**

___ **Breathe faster**

___ **Hard to pay attention**

___ **Talk faster**

___ **Mouth smiles**

___ **Heart pounds**

___ **Body shakes**

___ **Eye brows go up**

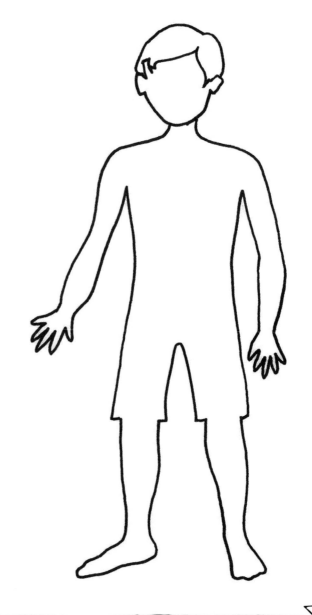

© Youthlight, Inc.

Ella's Excited Trivia

Ella "the excited" Elephant says....

1. It is normal to feel excited sometimes and not know why.

2. If you feel excited for too long, sometimes your stomach may hurt.

3. Animals like dogs can feel excited the same as people.

4. Sometimes people can make a mistake or forget to do something when they are excited.

5. When an excited person tells another person why they are excited, they can spread the excitement on to the other person like catching a cold.

6. There is always something you can do when you are excited to calm yourself down.

Feeling Excited? What Would You Do?

Lesson 21 Objective: Children will explore where and to what degree their feelings are in certain situations and ways to calm down.

Fill in the blanks and circle how much excitement you might feel based on the situation (use Appendix A & B).

1. **You just scored the winning goal in your soccer game.**

   How much excitement would you feel?   A little   A lot
   (Hint: On Appendix A – less than 5 = A little & more than 5 = A lot)

   Where would you feel it in your body? _____

   What would you do to help you calm down? _____
   _____

2. **Your parents surprised you with a trip to the amusement park.**

   How much excitement would you feel?   A little   A lot

   Where would you feel it in your body? _____

   What would you do to help you calm down? _____
   _____

3. **You just found 5 dollars on the ground.**

   How much excitement would you feel?   A little   A lot

   Where would you feel it in your body? _____

   What would you do to help you calm down? _____
   _____

Feeling Group 5: Relaxed

Lesson 22 Objective: Children will learn other names for the relaxed group feelings and to introduce the concept of different amounts of relaxation.

As Rusty surely knows, there are other feelings in the relaxed group that are similar to relaxed, just different amounts of relaxed. We can think of these feelings in terms of amounts from 0-10 where 10 is the most you have ever felt, 0 is none at all, and 5 is in the middle (see Appendix A).

Step 1: In the picture, find and color Rusty "the relaxed" Rabbit – he is a number 5!

Step 2: Now color in Rusty's friends and think about if they are more or less relaxed than Rusty. Look at their bodies. How can you tell if they are more or less relaxed than Rusty? (Hint: If their number is more than 5, they are more relaxed than Rusty. If their number is less than 5 they are less relaxed than Rusty.)

EXTRA CREDIT!! *If they are more relaxed, color them darker than Rusty by pressing harder. If they are less relaxed, color them lighter than Rusty by pressing lighter.*

Rhonda "the exhausted" Rabbit – I am a number 10

Richard "the calm" Rabbit – I am a number 3

Roxanne "the sleepy" Rabbit – I am a number 8

Robert "the tired" Rabbit – I am a number 7

What Does Relaxed Feel Like?

Hello kids, this is Rusty "the relaxed" Rabbit. When I am feeling relaxed, this is what it feels like in my body...

It feels slow like snails are under my paws.

It feels like something is pulling my ears to the ground.

It feels full like my stomach is full of grass and daisies.

It feels soft like I am lying on a bed of feathers.
(Draw a picture of this for Rusty below.)

What are the clues that you might be relaxed?
Rusty says that you can tell you might be relaxed by listening to your body clues. It is important to know if you are relaxed so you can get some rest if you need it.

Lesson 23 Objective: Children will learn to identify where on their body they may feel relaxation.

Step 1: Finish the sentence below

I felt relaxed when _____

Step 2: Draw in your relaxed face. Then check the body clues below if you think you felt it when you were relaxed.

Step 3: For each body clue checked, color and/or draw a line to where you think it might be on the picture to the right.

__ **Face/Body feels cooler**

__ **Breathe slower**

__ **Think more clearly**

__ **Talk slower**

__ **Eye lids droop or feel heavy**

__ **Heart slows down**

__ **Jaw loosens**

__ **Eye brows go down**

__ **Shoulders drop**

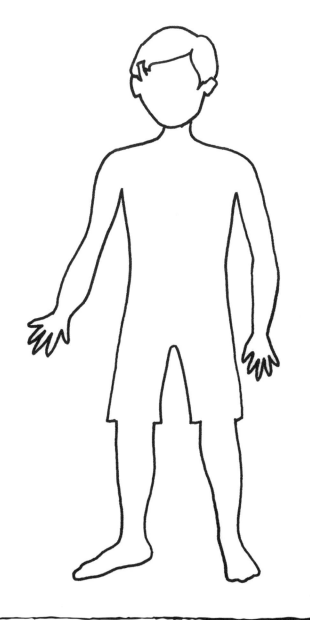

Rusty's Relaxed Trivia

Rusty "the relaxed" Rabbit says....

1. It is normal to feel relaxed sometimes and not know why.

2. If you feel relaxed for too long, it may mean something is wrong like you are sick or depressed.

3. Animals like dogs can feel relaxed the same as people.

4. Feeling relaxed is necessary so our bodies can rest and repair. That is why babies sleep up to 16 hours per day.

5. Relaxed & excited work together as a team, to bring you up and slow you down. You need both of them for your body to work right.

Feeling Relaxed?
What Would You Do?

Lesson 24 Objective: Children will explore where and to what degree their feelings are in certain situations and ways to feel better.

Fill in the blanks and circle how much relaxation you might feel based on the situation (use Appendix A & B).

1. You just ran a mile in gym class.

How much relaxation would you feel?   A little   A lot
(Hint: On Appendix A – less than 5 = A little & more than 5 = A lot)

Where would you feel it in your body? _____

What would you do to help you feel better? _____

_____

2. You stayed up all night doing a project for school.

How much relaxation would you feel?   A little   A lot

Where would you feel it in your body? _____

What would you do to help you feel better? _____

_____

3. You just finished eating a big bowl of pasta.

How much relaxation would you feel?   A little   A lot

Where would you feel it in your body? _____

What would you do to help you feel better? _____

_____

© Youthlight, Inc.

Congratulations! Now you know all about your feelings including where you feel them in your body and how much. Color in each feeling friend in the order listed: sad, mad, scared & relaxed.

Uh Oh....which one of our feeling friends is missing?

Now its time to learn what to do to help you deal with some of your feelings the right way!

Remember...all feelings are normal and everyone gets them sometimes. However, it is what you choose to do when you feel a certain way that can be right or wrong.

Feelings: Making a right or wrong choice?

Lesson 25 Objective: To help assess a child's ability to differentiate between right and wrong choices associated with a feeling.

1. You feel sad and talk to your parents about how you feel.
   Right?___   Wrong?___

2. You feel sad and punch your brother for teasing you.
   Right?___   Wrong?___

3. You feel angry and kick a hole in your wall.
   Right?___   Wrong?___

4. You feel angry and listen to your music in your room.
   Right?___   Wrong?___

5. You feel scared and write in a journal what you are scared about.
   Right?___   Wrong?___

6. You feel scared and start picking an argument with a friend.
   Right?___   Wrong?___

7. You get excited and run around the classroom when other students are trying to read silently.
   Right?___   Wrong?___

8. You feel relaxed and take a nap before dinner.
   Right?___   Wrong? ___

Right choices are often called Coping Skills. We use them to deal with our feelings when they become too difficult for us to handle. We know they are right choices by asking ourselves a question.

Will my choice hurt myself or anyone else?

Yes = Wrong choice   No = Right Choice

However even though we want to always make right choices, sometimes we make wrong choices when we are sad, mad, scared, relaxed and even excited.

Lesson 26 Objective: Children will identify wrong choices they have made in the past.

Draw a wrong choice you made when you felt _____ *(write in a feeling)*.

Lesson 27 Objective: Children will expand their understanding of the wrong choices they can make to deal with feelings.

Here's a list of some other wrong choices to deal with feelings. Have you ever done any of these? Circle Yes or No.

Slam doors	Yes	No
Yell at someone	Yes	No
Steal something	Yes	No
Stomp your feet	Yes	No
Try to hurt yourself	Yes	No
Run away	Yes	No
Hit someone	Yes	No
Kick someone	Yes	No
Throw things	Yes	No
Cuss	Yes	No
Hit someone in a private place	Yes	No
Not follow directions	Yes	No
Break something	Yes	No
Scream loudly	Yes	No
Say mean things to someone else	Yes	No
Refuse to answer someone	Yes	No
Other_____	Yes	No

Lesson 28 Objective: Children will learn the right choices they have made to deal with feelings.

Draw a time you made a right choice when you were feeling

_____
(write in feeling.)

Lesson 29 Objective: To expand upon a child's coping skill list.

Here is a list of some other right choices or coping skills that you can use when you are mad, sad, scared, excited or relaxed. Have you done any of these?

Step 1: Put a ✓ next to the ones you have tried.

Step 2: Circle 3 that you have not tried but you think may help you.

__ **Talk to some I trust about how I feel (I trust_____)**

__ **Draw a picture about how I feel**

__ **Do some activity like sports**

__ **Read a book**

__ **Organize something (like a deck of cards by suit)**

__ **Play with some of my toys**

__ **Clean my room**

__ **Run around my backyard**

__ **Write in a journal about how I feel**

__ **Drink a glass of water**

__ **Sing a song**

___ **Take a hot or cold shower**

___ **Write out the lyrics to a favorite song**

___ **Relax in my room**

___ **Count to 20** *(backwards if you can)*

___ **Breathing – 4-7-8 Breathe in for a 4 count
Hold for a 7 count
Breathe out for an 8 count**
(personal count not seconds)

___ **Play a musical instrument**

___ **Do a puzzle (crossword, word find, jigsaw)**

___ **Listen to music**

___ **Throw/bounce/kick a ball** *(foam ball if inside!!!)*

___ **Call a friend**

___ **Find a picture in a magazine and make up a story about it**
(you can draw or write the story down)

___ **Write a letter to god/person I love telling how I feel**

___ **Make up a new dance**

___ **Take a nap**

___ **Other** _____

My Healing Hand

Lesson 30 Objective: To increase a child's ability to choose healthy coping skills when feeling mad, sad or scared.

Step 1: Read the story from Appendix C aloud to the child choosing the applicable gender.

Step 2: Get a piece of posterboard and trace their hand in the middle. Decorate the posterboard as much as you like. Then have the child choose 5 right choices for dealing with their feelings. It is recommended one of the choices be an internal process like breathing that they can do anywhere, anytime without any materials. At the tip of each finger write the word(s) of the coping skill and paste an icon for the coping skill above the words. Place the healing hand somewhere it is easily accessible for them to read or look at. Then practice having your child try to remember what finger is what right choice.

Step 3: When they are giving signs of feeling a certain way, prompt them to choose something off their healing hand and do it. Check in with them later to see how and if it helped them feel better and reward accordingly for successes.

Note: An additional method is to get an old glove and hot glue the icons onto the fingers.

Dealing with Feelings: Putting It All Together

Lesson 31 Objective: Children will practice what they learned by responding to scenarios.

Read each scenario and answer the questions using the applicable appendices.

Scenario 1
Joshua has been waiting all weekend to go to the pool with his friend. When he sees his mother before she heads out the door he asks if he can go and she says he can't because he did not clean his room this morning.

1. How might Josh feel? _____

2. Where might he feel this in his body (use Appendix B)? _____

3. Use 2 words to describe this feeling (use Appendix B)? _____
   _____

4. How much is he feeling this feeling (use Appendix A)?
   _____

5. Pick one right choice he can make to help him deal with this feeling.
   _____

Scenario 2

Angela was recently adopted. She has been living with her new family for 6 months and has started to connect with them. One day her adopted mom tells her she will be flying out of town and will be gone for a week.

1. How might Angela feel? _____

2. Where might she feel this in her body (use Appendix B)? _____

3. Use 2 words to describe this feeling (use Appendix B). _____
   _____

4. How much is she feeling this feeling (use Appendix A)? _____
   _____

5. Pick one right choice she can make to help her deal with this feeling.
   _____

Scenario 3

Brandon returned home from school today with his parents waiting at the door. They ushered him into the house and had him sit on the couch. They told him that his grandmother had passed away.

1. How might Brandon feel? _____

2. Where might he feel this in his body (use Appendix B)? _____

3. Use 2 words to describe this feeling (use Appendix B)? _____
   _____

4. How much is he feeling this feeling (use Appendix A)?
   _____

6. Pick one right choice he can make to help him deal with this feeling.
   _____

Scenario 4

Madison has been studying for her spelling test all week. When she goes to school that Friday she takes the test and an hour later finds out she got the highest grade in the class.

1. How might Madison feel? _____

2. Where might she feel this in her body (use Appendix B)? _____

3. Use 2 words to describe this feeling (use Appendix B). _____
   _____

4. How much is she feeling this feeling (use Appendix A)?
   _____

5. Pick one right choice she can make to help her control this feeling.
   _____

Scenario 5

Caden has just finished basketball practice where the coach ran the team for over a hour straight.

1. How might Caden feel? _____

2. Where might he feel this in his body (use Appendix B)? _____

3. Use 2 words to describe this feeling (use Appendix B). _____
   _____

4. How much is he feeling this feeling (use Appendix A)?
   _____

5. Pick one right choice he can make to help him deal with this feeling.
   _____

Lesson 32 Objective: Children will use the symbol of a traffic light to understand and remember what concepts they learned in this book.

Use Appendix E: My Feelings Traffic Light. Make copies and have children first color their traffic light. Then have them answer the questions for each situation using their My Feelings Traffic Light.

1. One of the big kids in school steps on your new white sneakers on purpose.

2. After eating your entire dinner and a large helping of ice cream, you sit down on the couch to watch television.

3. You get lost at the park and cannot find your parents.

4. Your parents tell you that you are going to have a new baby brother.

5. Your little sister lies and tells your parents you did something you did not do.

6. Your parents got into an argument and were yelling at each other loudly.

7. Your soccer coach yells at you for not passing the ball.

8. Your sister got a new bicycle but you did not.

9. A kid in your class asks you to lie to the teacher about stealing something from her desk.

10. Describe something that happened at school this week.
    _____

11. Describe something that happened at home this week.
    _____

Hello kids...it's Rusty the "relaxed" Rabbit here. It is important to know that when something happens in our lives that we do not like or did not expect, there are a few things that can happen before and after we feel something to help us along. I like to think of it sort of like a train moving down a track from the caboose to the engine tooting E-F-A-O! That's short for Event-Feeling-Action-Outcome!

Take a look at Appendix F: My Feelings Train in the back of this book.

Here is what goes in each train car:

Caboose = Event or what happens

Car 1 = Feeling you get

Car 2 = Action you take or choice you make

Engine = Outcome or what happened because of the action you took

Lesson 33 Objective: To help children organize events related to feelings and behaviors sequentially.

Step 1: Make 4 copies of Appendix F: *My Feelings Train*.

Step 2: Put the list of events in order on the Appendix F: My Feelings Train by writing the bolded word in the correct train car window.

Step 3: After you write in the word, color the train the correct color based on whether it is the Event (Red) – Feeling (Yellow) – Action (Blue) – Outcome (Green).

1. Event ➜ Your **sister** gets to stay up late and you do not ➜ Color Red
   Feeling ➜ Feel **mad** in your chest ➜ Color Yellow
   Action ➜ Choose to **color** in your room ➜ Color Blue
   Outcome ➜ Feel **calm** ➜ Color Green

2. Outcome ➜ Feel **relaxed** ➜ Color Green
   Feeling ➜ Feel **angry** in your hands ➜ Color Yellow
   Event ➜ Someone **stole** your music player ➜ Color Red
   Action ➜ Choose to tell the **teacher** ➜ Color Blue

Now try it without the E-F-A-O helping words! Write them in if you know the answer!

3. _____ A **bully** threatens to beat you up at recess ➜ Color Red
   _____ Feel **safer** ➜ Color Green
   _____ Feel **scared** in your heart ➜ Color Yellow
   _____ Choose to tell the **principal** ➜ Color Blue

4. _____ Write a **letter** about how you are feeling ➜ Color Blue
   _____ You found out your **dog** died ➜ Color Red
   _____ Feel less **sad** ➜ Color Green
   _____ Feel **distraught** in your face and heart ➜ Color Yellow

Feelings Word Search

S	B	D	E	T	A	R	T	S	U	R	F
B	L	E	R	A	G	E	T	N	L	E	E
O	D	L	D	F	E	E	L	I	N	G	S
D	Q	R	I	P	F	E	H	E	L	E	R
Y	R	D	E	K	A	R	R	K	C	G	F
E	A	E	D	L	S	U	O	V	R	E	N
T	A	A	E	R	A	G	N	A	E	K	O
R	S	H	T	Y	R	X	N	F	Y	T	R
E	Y	E	I	A	R	N	E	I	P	I	M
G	T	M	C	R	E	A	M	D	P	F	L
N	N	A	X	F	R	T	G	N	A	O	A
A	L	D	E	R	A	C	S	E	H	C	C

Calm Frustrated Coping Skills Rage Nervous
Happy Body Scared Anger Feelings
Mad Sad Excited Relaxed Fear

Feelings Crossword

Across

1. Rusty the "_____" Rabbit
2. C_____S_____ help us deal with our feelings the right way
3. Marvin the "_____" Moose
4. Ella the "_____" Elephant
5. Sammy's friend Sally the "_____" sheep – I am a number 3
6. All feelings are _____ and everyone gets them sometimes
7. When you feel angry you can make a right or _____ choice

Down

8. Marvin's friend Mason the "_____" Moose – I am a number 8
9. Sara the "_____" Seahorse
10. Harriet or Henry and the _____ hand – helps you make the right choice
11. Sammy the "_____" Sheep
12. When you have a feeling, you feel it on or inside your _____

Answers on page 102

True or False Anger Quiz

1. Anger always covers up some other emotion or feeling. _____

2. Other people can make you mad. _____

3. Feeling mad is different from feeling angry by how much you feel. _____

4. People who are sad, lonely and keep to themselves can be angry inside.
   _____

5. Once you are angry, there is no way to calm yourself down. _____

6. The feeling anger most often covers up is fear or being scared. _____

7. Every time you get angry, it is somehow connected to your past experiences.
   _____

8. Coping skills don't work to calm you down when you are frustrated.
   _____

9. Feeling frustrated or angry is normal. _____

10. If you are an angry person, you will be that way your whole life. _____

Answers on page 102

© Youthlight, Inc.

Feelings Quiz

Circle the correct answer

1. Another feeling in the sad group is..?

   A) Angry   B) Depressed   C) Exhausted   D) Happy

2. It is a right choice to stomp your feel when you are angry.

   A) True   B) False

3. If you are scared, you might feel it most in this part of your body.

   A) knees   B) elbows   C) heart   D) hair

4. Other people can make us mad by what they say or do.

   A) True   B) False

5. Another feeling in the excited group is..?

   A) Sad   B) Rage   C) Terrified   D) Elated

6. On a scale of 1-10, what number represents feeling a small amount of that feeling?

   A) 10   B) 1   C) 5   D) 8

7. All feelings are normal and everyone gets them sometimes.

   A) True   B) False

Answers on page 102

Activity 1: Movie Night

Recommended Grades: K-5

Materials: Computer, projector or TV, DVD player. Any children's movie (s), crayons, pencils, copy of Appendix A & B and Movie Night Worksheet (following page).

Overview: Using movie media to draw comparisons between where movie characters feel things in their bodies and where the students feel things in their bodies.

Objectives: To emphasize the understanding of where and how much a person feels things as well as to help children relate feelings to socially acceptable, non-threatening media.

Procedures: Distribute copies of Appendix A & B and the Movie Night Worksheet (next page) to each student. Divide the children into groups. Assign a feeling to each group (you must watch the movie before hand to pick these). Play scenes from a children's movie and pause the movie exactly on the point where one of the characters feels the certain feeling you assigned (you may need more than one set of AV equipment to do this in a timely way). Have students fill out the worksheet and color in the appropriate areas on Appendix A & B. Discuss as a class at the end?

Discussion Questions: Where do you feel that feeling in your body? How strong was that feeling? What did you do to make that feeling get to 0 or 1 (refer to Appendix A)? What did the character do?

Movie Night Worksheet

1. Groups assigned feeling _____

2. Name of character who feels the above feeling _____

3. What signs on the character's body tell you they feel this way? _____
   _____

4. How strong is this feeling (use Appendix A)? _____

5. Have you ever felt this way? _____

6. Describe this situation _____
   _____
   _____

7. Where did you feel this feeling in your body (use Appendix B)?
   _____

8. How strong was this feeling (use Appendix A)? _____

9. Did you do anything to lessen this feeling or make it go away?
   If so what did you do? _____
   _____
   _____

10. Did the movie character do anything to lessen or make the feeling go away?
    If so, what did they do? _____
    _____

© Youthlight, Inc.

Activity 2: Magazine Magic

Recommended Grades: 2-5

Materials: Magazines, scissors, glue, photocopy of Appendix A & B if needed, blank paper/construction paper.

Overview: Helping children create a story full of feelings using magazine pictures.

Objectives: To foster a child's creativity related to feelings and social situations. To help children process the big 5 feelings groups and gain greater understanding of how feelings are used in social situations.

Procedures: Divide into groups if desired. This can also be done as an individual project. Assign one of the 5 main feelings and have children construct a story with pictures from the magazines about that feeling. Have them tell the story about their picture to the other groups/students.

Discussion Questions: How did they feel when making up their story? Where did they feel while making their story? When have they ever felt this way? What did/can they do to change their feeling?

Activity 3: Picture Day

Recommended Grades: 1-5

Materials: Photographs from home. Photocopy of Appendix A, B, C. Crayons/Markers/Pencils

Overview: Using real life pictures to evaluate where people feel things in their bodies and how much.

Objectives: To emphasize the understanding of where and how much a person feels things. To help children notice how often people are feeling things in pictures.

Procedures: Have children go home and ask parents to get a picture of someone in the family feeling an emotion and bring it into school. On "Picture Day" distribute handouts of Appendix A, B, & C. Have children use Appendix A & B to write in how the person feels in the picture, where they feel it, what it feels like and how much. Then you can have them share with the class. They can also use Appendix C if they bring in a picture of someone who is angry.

Discussion Questions: Did anyone find a picture where someone was not feeling something? If there was more than one person in the picture, were they feeling the same thing or something different? How can you tell on their bodies?

Activity 4: New Feelings Practice

Recommended Grades: 2-5

Materials: Photocopy of Appendix A, B, C and E, pencil/marker or crayon. New Feelings Practice Worksheet (next page).

Overview: This activity will help children expand on what they have learned about feelings by introducing new feelings not directly addressed in this book.

Objectives: To organize the information learned about feelings into a process to better help children cope with stress and feelings encountered in their lives. To get them to extrapolate information learned about basic feelings to other feelings and situations.

Procedures: Have children complete My New Feelings Worksheet using applicable appendices if necessary. Process with the class if desired.

Discussion Questions: Was the feeling you had normal? Was the choice you made wrong or right? Could the feeling fit in more than one of the big 5 feeling groups? If so, which ones?

My New Feelings Worksheet

1. Pick and circle one of the following new feelings and answer the questions below.

Jealous   **Shy**   **Cautious**   **Discouraged**   **Confident**   **Embarrassed**

2. In which of the big 5 feelings groups do you think this feeling would go?
_____

3. Have you ever felt this feeling? If so, when? _____
_____

4. Where did you feel it in your body? _____

5. How much did you feel the feeling? _____

6. Did you do anything to help you deal with or show the feeling? If yes, what?
_____

7. If not, what could you have done to deal with this feeling? _____
_____

Activity 5: Touchy Feely

Recommended Grades: K-5

Materials: Any substance that has texture and temperature to it (i.e. pudding, beads, olive oil, sandpaper). Photocopy of Appendix B, pencil/crayon/marker, paper towels.

Overview: Used to help children develop greater understanding and awareness of the complexity of feelings in a fun and creative way.

Procedures: Have stations set up with different substances at each. Each child gets a turn feeling the substance and then using Appendix B (bottom) to note how that substance feels. For younger children the choices may need to be read to them.

Discussion Questions: Were you able to describe every substance? Can everything be described this way? Which feeling is like the pudding/oil/sandpaper etc?

Activity 6: Feelings Collage

Recommended Grades: 3-5

Materials: Scrap magazines, glue, scissors, construction paper/posterboard, pencils, crayons, markers.

Overview: Repeated emphasis on the non-verbal aspects of feelings helps improve children's sense of awareness of feelings in self and others and translates to greater degrees of empathy.

Objectives: To help children focus on the non-verbal aspects of different feelings.

Procedures: Divide class into 5 groups and assign one of the big 5 feelings to each group. Instruct them to keep it secret from the other groups. Have children cut and paste pictures (not words or letters) from the magazines creating a collage that reflects their feeling. Verbal assistance may be given helping the children find pictures where the persons/character's body seems to show that particular feeling may be helpful. After the groups have created their collages, they may get up and present their collage having the other groups try to guess their group's feeling.

For more advanced learning you may want to assign more complicated "in-between" feelings or alternate levels of one of the big 5 feelings.

Discussion Questions: What specific pictures in each collage helped people figure out the feeling? Were there any pictures where you could not tell how the character or person was feeling?

Activity 7: Feel The Music

Recommended Grades: 3-5

Materials: Photocopies of Appendix A & B (multiples for each sound/song), pencil/marker or crayon. (Laminated versions work better and can be reused over and over with dry erase markers), CD with sounds or different CD's with a variety of types of music.

Overview: Music, as one of the 5 senses, has a powerful ability to evoke particular affective states.

Objectives: To help children notice how different sounds can make them feel different things in their body.

Procedures: Distribute handouts and writing materials. Instruct children to sit in a comfortable position and note you will be playing a sound/song one at a time. Instruct them to notice how the "music" makes them feel and where they feel this in their body. Instruct them to fill out Appendix A & B accordingly.

Discussion Questions: How did the fast music make people feel? How may that be different from the slow or soft music? Did different people feel differently about the same sounds or music and is that normal?

Activity 8: Feelings Charades

Recommended Grades: 3-5

Materials: Charade Cards (next page).

Overview: Children need a great deal of practice and repetition associating feelings with non-verbal body signs so as to increase their awareness of those signs within themselves.

Objectives: To increase children's awareness of non-verbal body signs associated with particular feelings.

Procedures: Divide the class into two groups. Have each group select a player to go first and have one of them pick a charade card and show it to the other player. Then have them act out the character and the feeling using the standard rules for charades.

Discussion Questions: Were their any characters that had a feeling you wouldn't have guessed for them? Did that make it harder to act out or guess?

Charade Cards

Exhausted Santa Claus	Terrified Beetle	Lonely Grizzly Bear	Depressed Police Officer
Calm Bumble Bee	Frightened Elf	Distraught Surfer	Raging Chihuahua
Nervous Doctor	Elated Snake	Disappointed Easter Bunny	Tired Owl

Activity 9: Build A Feeling

Recommended Grades: 2-5

Materials: Clay, popsicle sticks, styrofoam packing materials, beads and any other building materials you can think of. You can even get some of this from a natural source such as tree bark, grass clippings, twigs, pine cones etc. Markers, crayons, scissors, glue.

Overview: Children are amazingly creative at how they would symbolically express feelings.

Objectives: To support and encourage children's creativity and subsequent abstract thoughts associated with feelings.

Procedures: Have children pick one of the big 5 feelings randomly. Instruct them to use the building materials to create a sculpture of the feeling and what it means to them.

Discussion Questions: Each child can describe their sculptured feeling to the other children in the class.

Appendix A
My Feelings Chart

Feeling: _____

Where in MY BODY: _____

HOW MUCH ⇨ Choose a number ⇨ Color in the heart for that number

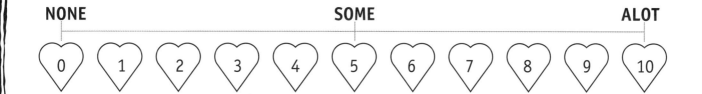

Appendix B
Where I Feel Things in My Body

Feeling: _____

Draw in your feeling face. Then draw/color the place where you feel this in or on your body.

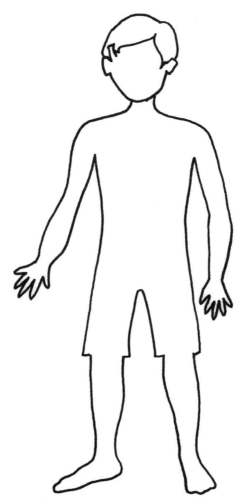

Pick from the list how this feels in your body

Hot or Cold	Soft or Hard	Rough or Smooth	Big or Small
Slow or Fast	Full or Empty	Loose or Tight	Sharp or Dull
Pushing or Pulling	Burning or Itching	Heavy or Light	Busy or Calm
Clean or Dirty	Strong or Weak	Dark or Light	High or Low

© Youthlight, Inc.

Appendix C
Anger Thermometer

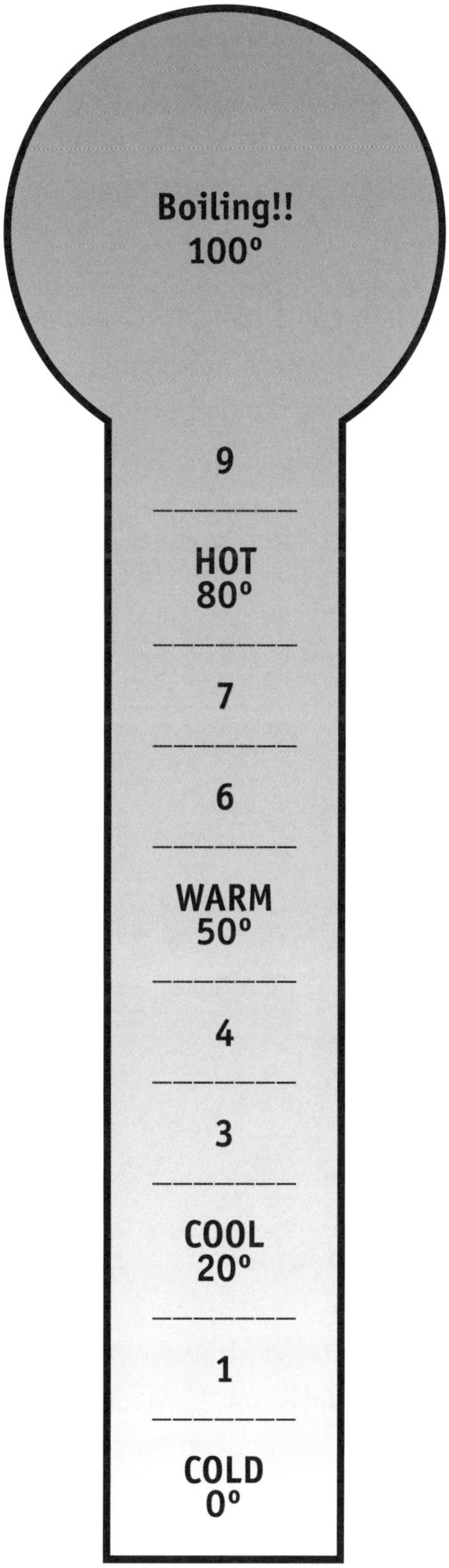

Boiling!!
100°

9

HOT
80°

7

6

WARM
50°

4

3

COOL
20°

1

COLD
0°

Appendix D
Henry (Harriet) and the Healing Hand

Once upon a time in a far away town lived a boy named Henry. Henry was a small boy of about the age of 10, yet his heart was as big as the sun itself and it shown most of the time just as brightly. But sometimes the light from Henry's heart was covered up by his grey, oversized hand. For as long as Henry could remember, his hands and the hands of others seemed to do bad things; always seemed to hurt.

Henry remembered the times when dad's hand hit mom in the face. He remembered when the police came and put dad's hands in handcuffs and took him away. This made Henry very sad. Now, mom and Henry's hands both seemed to be grey and full of sorrow.

"Henry, if I have to tell you one more time to clean up your room so help me I'll……" said his mother.

Henry's hands didn't like to clean up his room; they liked to do other bad things. Often, when Henry was alone and his hands had the chance, they liked to take things that did not belong to him. He would eventually get caught, and as always, there would be mother's big grey hand pointing out what he did wrong. As long as Henry could remember, HANDS, his and his parents, did only bad things and meant only sadness.

One day Henry went for a walk to his favorite tree and climbed up high to see as far as he could. It was a big oak tree that had lived there long before Henry was even born.

"Hello there," said a voice. Henry, startled, almost lost his grip and fell to the ground. He turned around only to see a large owl, perched high on the branch a few feet away.

"Hello there," tried the owl again. "How are you today?"

Henry, who was slightly afraid, replied "You can talk?"

"Of course I can talk," said Owl. "If you listen hard enough, all animals talk. I noticed your grey hand, what is the matter with it?" asked Owl.

Henry replied, "It's been that way for as long as I can remember. My hands always seem to do bad things."

"Well, if it's only your hand and not your heart, let's see if we can't change that! Follow me." said Owl.

And with one swift motion of his wings, Owl flew off and began to circle high above the oak tree. "Come, follow me!" Owl called again as he flew high into the blue sky.

Henry climbed down from the tree and followed the owl far and wide across the grass, across the farms and along the side of a river bank to a place Henry had never been before. Owl waddled over to a smaller tree near the river bank and motioned with his wing for Henry to follow him.

"Take it out" beckoned Owl. There, in the hollow of the tree was a wooden box that looked as ancient as the tree itself.

"Take it out and open it," Owl coaxed again.

Henry, a bit scared, took the box from the tree and slowly creaked opened the lid. In the center of the box was what appeared to be an old glove that had been used for many years. It was dirty, dull and looked too big for Henry's hand. What did he need a dirty old glove for anyway? Mom had just bought him a new pair this winter.

"I don't need a new glove, thanks anyway," said Henry.

"Oh, this is no ordinary glove," winked Owl. "It's the Healing Hand."

"The Healing Hand? What's that?" asked Henry with new curiosity.

"The Healing Hand is a special glove, given only to children who have a golden heart. When you feel sad or scared, the Healing Hand helps remind you what you can do to feel better. Go ahead. Put it on." encouraged Owl.

"But I can't wear a dirty old glove on my hand all day. My mom will yell at me," Henry stammered.

"Just put it on and you will see. The glove only works for kids whose hearts are true, and I can see you have a true heart." said owl.

So Henry reached into the box and picked up the ratty old glove. When he put it on, to his surprise, the glove seemed to change size and colors, and melted right into his hand. His hand seemed to change colors too and wasn't grey anymore!

"Now, think about something sad or a time when you felt angry," whispered Owl.

So Henry began thinking about the times his father had hit his mother. Suddenly on the tips of his fingers there appeared pictures of things Henry loved to do that always made him feel better. On his thumb appeared a set of crayons because Henry loved to color. On his pointer finger was an image of him kicking a ball. On his middle finger there was a radio, because he loved music. On his ring finger, there were some of his toys and on his pinky was the smiling face of his best friend whom he loved to talk with.

"Remember," announced Owl, "As long as your heart stays true and golden, your healing hand will always help you find a way not to feel and act so grey." And with that final clue, in one large swooping motion and the wink of a wise eye, Owl flew far away.

Over the next few years Henry continued to use his Healing Hand every time he was scared, angry or nervous. It always helped him feel better to pick one of the things his hand suggested, many of which were fun. Ever since the day he climbed the tree, met Owl, and put on the dirty glove, his hand was never grey again.

Appendix E
My Feelings Traffic Light

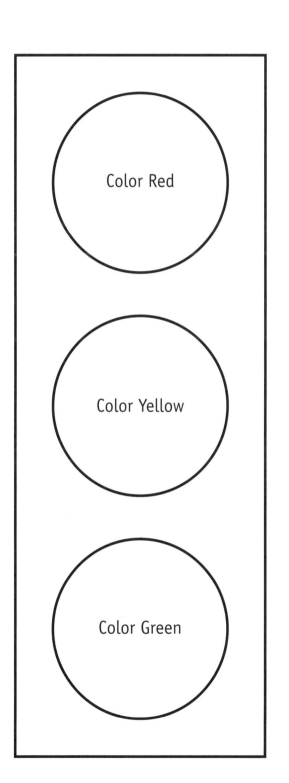

○ **STOP** - Describe the situation- What happened?

○ Tell how you feel & where you feel it in your body!

○ Pick one thing you can do to help you feel better
or
ask for what you need!

© Youthlight, Inc.

Appendix F
My Feelings Train

Step 1: Color in the Caboose red

Step 2: Color in the 1st box car yellow

Step 3: Color in the 2nd box car blue

Step 4: Color in the Engine Green

Now you are ready to go!!

Answers To Crossword & Quizzes

Crossword

Across
1. relaxed
2. coping skills
3. mad
4. excited
5. lonely
6. normal
7. wrong

Down
8. angry
9. scared
10. healing
11. sad
12. body

Anger True/False Anger Quiz
1. True
2. False
3. True
4. True
5. False
6. True
7. True
8. False
9. True
10. False

Feelings Quiz
1. B
2. B
3. C
4. B
5. D
6. B
7. A

About the Author

Aaron is a licensed professional counselor and has been practicing in the Denver, Colorado area since 1998. A specialist in the area of trauma, attachment and adoption, Aaron uses a unique approach to connecting with children and families to help them deal with the brokenness of their lives. This workbook arose out of the understanding that many children he was working with, especially those who had experienced trauma, had poor understanding of true feelings and emotion, and that this was inhibiting their healing. It is hoped this workbook will be used as a practical guide to help children and their families understand how and "where" they feel throughout the country.

About the Illustrator

Karla Trapp M.A. has a Master's Degree in Transpersonal Counseling and Art Therapy from Naropa University, and currently works in a private practice with children. She has worked with trauma and grief in children extensively. She lives with her husband and two children in Denver, Colorado. More on Karla and her artwork can be found at www.art-alchemy.com.

You can contact the author at:
aaronlpc@gmail.com or by mail at:

High Mountain Counseling LLC
P.O. Box 261329
Lakewood, CO 80226

You can also visit his website at:

www.allabouttrauma.com

References

Bessel A. Van Der Kolk M.D. (2004) Trauma and Memory. *Psychiatry and Clinical Neurosciences. (52)*, (5), 97-109.

Bremner J. D., Randall P., Vermetten E, Staib L., Bronen R.A., Mazure C. M., Capelli S., McCarthy G., Innis R. B., Charney D.S. (1997): MRI-based measurement of hippocampal volume in post traumatic stress disorder related to childhood physical and sexual abuse: A preliminary report. *Biological Psychiatry (41)*:23-32.

Deangelis, Tori (2007). A new diagnosis for childhood trauma? *Monitor on Psychology (38)*, (3). 32.

De Bellis, M.D., Chrousos, G. P., Dorn, L. D., Burke, L., Helmers, K., Kling, M. A., Trickett, P. K., & Putnam, F. W. (1994). Hypothalamic-pituitary-adrenal axis dysregulation in sexually abused girls. *Journal of Clinical Endocrinology & Metabolism, (78)(2)*, 249-55.

Doka, Kenneth & Martin, Terry (2000) Men *Don't Cry . . . Women Do: Transcending Gender Stereotypes of Grief.*

Trauma, Brain & Relationship – Helping Children Heal (2004) Santa Barbara Graduate Institute.

Volpicelli, Joseph, M.D., PhD., Balaraman, Geetha, Hahn, Julie, Wallace, Heather, M.A., and Bux, Donald, PhD. (1999). The Role of Uncontrollable Trauma in the Development of PTSD and Alcohol Addiction. *Alcohol Research and Health (23)(4)*, 256, 26.